Signals

Sumeet Grover

Smallberry Press

A CIP catalogue record of this book is available from the British Library. ISBN: 978-0-9930315-2-6

Published by Smallberry Press, International House, 24 Holborn Viaduct, London EC1A 2BN. www.smallberrypress.co.uk

Front cover image copyright Kuco/Shutterstock.com

When all becomes silent,

one must hear within

CONTENTS

Silence   1

Longing for Rafael   2

Monochrome   4

Uneasy   6

Milk   7

Sleep   8

Nowhere   9

Fourteen   11

Late from work   12

Bruised   13

Relentless   14

Now   15

Vacant   17

The Jungian Analyst   18

Woman   20

Religion   21

Blankness   23

Hell	24
Enough Money	25
Sycamores	27
Home	28
Nothing New	29
Oona's Mum	31
Signals	34
Asleep	36
Nothingness	37
Dorothy Livesay	38
Thirty Three	39
Unimportant	41
Deep	42
Finding	43
Stopping	45
Counting Coins	46
Forty Seven	47
Looking	48
Shoulder	49
Tomorrow	51
Touch	52

Jewellery	53
Weak	54
Late	55
Emptiness	57
Loss	58
Counting	59
Coffee Date	60

Silence

In silence there is
no expectation, no demand,
no scrutiny.

In silence there is
no shame, no fear, no hesitation,
no need for repair.

If silence is all there is,
it is all the permission I need

to think, to speak, to express, to imagine,
to walk, to sit, to weep, to hope.

Longing for Rafael

After eating chicken and aubergines, turned cold
by our autumn breath from endless talk,
waiters reluctant of pouring free water in your
empty glass, we went out for an afternoon walk.

Cold blood paused beneath my skin:
you clasped my hand, warmed me as we
walked on stony pavement under silver air.
You said one day we will have children, three,
and I named them Rafael, Zoya and Zaakir.

Zoya and Zaakir chose to live with me
and you went away with Rafael.
You were reluctant to choose middle names,
all in English, all in your language, and so
as I fill in school forms, their names are still
like your empty glass that afternoon.

To imagine Zoya is a dilemma: she is a girl and
in my city where I once was a boy, girls
had their hands tied in magenta glass bangles
and yellow nylon ropes that people used
to hang laundry in their courtyards.

But I always think of Zaakir, he
jumps out of me every time I see
a ginger sponge cake; he also has your
green eyes, although some times with your
water colours he brushes them grey.

I have lived with our children who were
born in our pointless thinking that evening at the
decline of November, but I long to see
Rafael, his honey-brown skin and how tall is he.

I get visions of him running in the
wilderness of Hornby, pulling spring leaves
from alder and maple trees,
picking mahonia and salmonberries.

That evening as we spoke, as we dreamed,
we created three children, and soon parted ways:
you with one and two with me.

I am longing to see my second son;
I am longing for Rafael.

Monochrome

Always on the wide walnut wood
table behind his bed: framed in black,
a five by six monochrome photo
of his mother from '66, the year
he was born.

A zigzag aluminium stem stretching out
from white wall behind, ending into
a conelamp above his bed: his late morning
sun on Saturdays and Sundays, two
work days.

When he spoke, he spoke
all things silly.

- Why can't you see your eyebrows?

What you see in my face
is what you want to believe.

Numbers zero and seven printed
on a spiral staircase painting:
what did the artist mean? –

He spoke of most things, but never more
than the year of that monochrome photo
of his mother;

never said who she was, except memory
of her lemon cake on a Winnipeg camping
trip in '83 with three brothers and
twin sisters.

Many recollections of Uncle Billy:
she named him after her brother;
no more a word about her.

Uneasy

Fluffy rice cakes being formed
by steam contained in steel
cooker as it whistles.

Uneasy vapours arrogant in energy,
smelling strongly, unapologetic
like an adolescent, pound
uneven cooker on flat
electric stove.

He leans on kitchen counter,
glares at glass stove, and he
doesn't know when he became
resentful of being touched on his chest.

Milk

Four days old. In afternoon daylight,
the baby suckles Farha's right breast;

she smiles at Estella: new to her name,
new to her older cousin's clothes, new to this home

where cash is scarce but ambitions are many.
Her father restless, pulls out kitchen drawers,

searches beneath shoes, searches pockets
of loose fit jeans from Sunday market sale.

What is it? I ask. *"A ten pound voucher...
received it in post; give me few minutes,*

*and then we go
to buy her milk from the Romanian store."*

Sleep

Sleep   tonight
is in a pruned country field,
her breath I cannot feel.

Sleep   tonight
is an unknown lover,
a man I have never seen.

Sleep   tonight
is a sentence on bed;
eyes open,
unwilling to dream.

Nowhere

You can hear the clatter ten
feet away, one bedroom away
at seven-ten after daybreak as
she mixes sugar in cardamom *chai*
with a steel spoon in a
dark blue mug her son left
last time he came home.

Shaila stands barefooted
on marble floor, she stands
under white light not so dim,
so that aged seventy-six
she would need no glasses to see
dishes stacked in steel sink,
tomato stains on beige tiles,
purple tumblers covered in dust,
green light on water filter blinking,
red onions in the basket rotten.

"Who will come to visit us?
I wipe those glasses when someone does."
The tea is ready, she clutches her mug,
walks steadily; still wearing the night gown,

sits on brown settee and drinks
through brushed dentures,
relishing every sip, looking
nowhere.

Fourteen

He licks ice cream, northern
summer too feeble to melt it;
his grey shorts folded to
half the length of his thighs.
Skin hairless like a younger
boy's plump cheeks;
he is still fourteen.

White t-shirt and black goggles,
he comes home with some DVDs;
spends most days in his room
at the PC except when daddy
shouts *the meal is ready.*

Never a letter   from mummy.

Late from work

When she laughs she doesn't know
how loud, how creaky her voice.

She is often the only person
laughing when she laughs.

She cuts vegetables on kitchen counter:
cuts aubergines, cuts courgettes.

Cuts them with a salad knife, smaller
than her vegetables; drops them in a pan.

Watches afternoon soaps on TV, naps;
waits for her husband to return.

Cuts his blazers, cuts his arms on
evenings when he's late from work.

Bruised

He tears off linen shorts,
drags down underpants, front
body pressed against carpet;
lashes on the butt,
becomes bruised.

He does it to himself before
someone else does it;
he does it to his son so that
no one else does it.

Family is a poison, when
it hits inside the body,
it keeps on hitting;
it doesn't stop.

Relentless

She nurses the child, her face
pale, eyes empty of expression:
she looks at the infant and smiles.

The duty on her lap is relentless:
babies demand breasts more often
than a woman can fill herself.

She smiles, she smiles
before tears break peace:
motherhood is a slow demise.

Now

Now cannot be touched:
it has no form.

Now cannot be counted:
iron clock-ticks know
nothing of its velocity.

Now is the stillness
of this body as its
heart races.

Now comes; Now evades.
It re-enters the body
from nose to the stomach.

Now is in my breath:
fulfilling and emptying.

Now is emptiness:
even when it fills,
it cannot be seen.

Now has no form,
yet it is here.

Vacant

So vacant his life, so lone
in his errands, only him
who opens the main door;
soundless house where surrealist
canvases are memories.

No mention of friends,
no plan on his mind;
I watch him stand under the
kitchen light: self-absorbed,
anxious arms, as he marinates
za'atar chicken, roasts red peppers;
afraid   to let tears run free
and to answer my question why he
never lived with someone.

Books, too many of them
and a landline, and sometimes
soft white chrysanthemums
absorbing water, yet fading by
the burning light.

The Jungian Analyst

Too much of herself in that
sitting room:

lines etched on a bronze metal painting;
portrait of a nineteenth century
important woman; three hundred
books on religion, on soul, on neuroses
positioned in discipline; sculpture
of a white man   looking inwards;

pashmina shawl from Delhi spread
over her legs as she would have lain on the chaise:
a hundred years ago it would have been
a patient's couch, telling her analyst
she felt guilty as she feels aroused by him.

Rough, caramel shaded leather flakes
would fall from armrest of the
sofa where I sat; I tried to
think of analysands who sat there over
forty years: many of them she must have
called neurotic, laughed with privilege, and
told them their misery is fantasy.

Too much of herself in that
sitting room: I would hear her tell me
of my rage, my hatred of people, of how
deaf to the crowds I was.

When for the last evening I went,
she hoped that the man,
that man   whom I
denounced for two months in obsession,
would fade away from my memory.

"Which man?" I asked, and she
didn't know; neither did I.

The white man, sculptured, looking
inwards in pain   kept on looking.
I left.

Woman

Woman: that word means more than
female; no one would admit it.

Woman: some men are, woman,
we call them so, look down
on them with disgust, resentment
that they refuse to behave
as we say, rage that they
see skinny jeans, scented candles,
face creams, chrysanthemums
and paintings as just things.

Woman: I am a weary man convicted
of being woman. I burn every word,
every sentence: my spirit runs free.

Religion

You say there is a
single truth, a single faith
that will awaken, lead all
to joy, lead all to fulfilment.

You say the Buddha
wrote this truth, and he
was the single person to
discover it.

You say for a Buddhist
to think differently
is betrayal, misfortune
will descend.

You say a single scripture
is supreme in thought,
it is supreme in promise
and all else is folly.

You pity the Christians,
the Jews, the Muslims;
you reprimand Hindus with

multiple gods, you ignore Greeks.

I say to you turn back
the clock, flip back the
sheets of a calendar until
it is June four years ago.

It has been three hours:
Darioush lies on bed,
his face locked in polythene,
his arteries thirsty
for an arrest.

I say to you to whisper
through that polythene bag:
"there is a single truth,
a single faith,
a single scripture."

Darioush will leave you,
he will leave me
and he will leave all
truths in thirty minutes.

Blankness

He rings the bell observantly
at four pm; never forgets his troubles,
and never any instructions.

Two floors above, walks up the steps
wearing polished black shoes,
laces held tight in the bow; takes

two minutes each time
looking at paintings:
white walls in that analytical room
have never known blankness.

Blankness: he was blank once,
it is a disease where you fail
in everything you do, even to
end it.

Hell

Clara walks her boy to school, he says
many times: *"Mummy, I love you"*
before his teacher takes him away.

At home she opens her book of religion,
places it with love on her lap.
In the quiet of a day with no end,
she reads; later cooks beef, bakes
a sponge cake, eats and telephones

job centre man, street cleaning
department at the local government,
electrician, superstore helpline and
returns woman at the mail order company,
and questions them:

"You, you and you and you,
what has Jesus done to you?
I hear your voice, I imagine your face.
Heaven is a lie, his love is disgrace.
Give me a better service next time,
we all go to hell anyway."

Enough Money

In evenings when back home
from work, he often stands
on the patio, looks far above
white crown of the gazebo;
holds a bowl full of fennel seeds
in his hand with a pewter spoon.

He smokes away his feelings,
smokes away despair,
smokes away all troubles;
chews fennel seeds and smokes,
smokes those cigarettes
till he knows the cost of
tobacco has
slapped the daily budget.

At nine o'clock in evenings he
goes to sleep whilst his wife
soothes a crying infant: hungry,
angry for a touch.

He sleeps away like he smokes;
wakes up from the morning alarm.

Another evening, another night
passes away; there is
just enough money
to keep that house running.

Sycamores

A pigeon has flown above a muddy terrace,
its feet now grip bark on a sycamore tree.

I watch fifty pigeons flutter on Sunday afternoons
after they have dirtied neighbourhood balconies;

they all find sycamores, they all find bark
to land, to grip and to behold silver suburban skies.

I am yet to find a sycamore, bark to grip:
today again I have been deprived of silver sight.

Home

the stranger in your home
comes everyday;
mama tells you, her room
is where he stays.

the stranger in your home
doesn't speak; he speaks
only when he beats.

the stranger in your home
is your father you are told;
the stranger in your home
doesn't go away.

Nothing New

You are always *fine*, as though
my telephone line has frozen in time.
For two years and more, you have said:
"All is normal, there is nothing new...
So what about you?"

Last week I spoke at a university
about a woman in Bhopal, about some people
whose homes we once found unnecessary.
Next month I recite my poems in a library:
read history I documented, read lives I witnessed.

Thirty-one years, I am still besotted with
native food: two fried *samosas* this morning.

Spent hours this week browsing catalogues
of fabrics from a First Nations shop;
spent weeks pondering what is time,
what is now, what is me, what is present
and what will come. I couldn't think of you;
you are always *fine*, you say

"All is normal, there is nothing new..."

My telephone line, the impatience to tell you things,
the wait to hear from you, all
have frozen in time.

This distance that exists, this space that is
between you and I: it once united us.
But for two years and more, all that was normal,
all that was nothing new separates us.

Oona's Mum

– What is that philosophy book you were reading?
Have you written something new? Five days
I didn't hear a word... what about your local
peace group? Be gentle, do not criticise them,
they will realise one day –

A postcard arrives, stamped from Victoria post office:
at the bottom it reads – *Oona's Mum* – Along with it
another packet; I tear brown paper and there is a thick
hand cut card, its edges at places narrowing like London
roads where cyclists and cars and buses converge.

In the card, leaves glued from fern, Garry oak, arbutus
and other trees, and her writing next to these reads
– they are all native to the west coast –
like First Nations children who were snatched from
their homes by the federal government between
1840 to 1990s.

I write to her every week, but nine days now
I had nothing to speak. Her cards, her parcels
always swift: in three days they travel from BC to
London, now in my post box; opened it before

climbing up the seventh floor
after a crowded humid day in the city.

– This is the last message I write...
Off to Cumberland soon to watch
descendants of miners sing aloud, read verses
and lay roses on miners' graves.
No access to telephone or computer...
no access to the outside world –

Six days pass and I wonder what I will write
in my next letter, unopened when she switches on
her computer in the study room where she
– can see the USA from the window –

Perhaps I should write I have stopped doing letters:
words are not noisy they don't travel
past my front door, they are cheap, they are worthless,
they are ignored.

Spent two weeks writing letters to journalists
of left and centre, telling them of the epidemic in India:
"You report about rape but no one utters a word
about Taara who is beaten every night in Delhi
by her husband and in mornings she walks her
daughter to school."

Only if my alphabets were as swift
as Victoria post from BC to London; only if a beaten
mother and a child were more important than an
A-list celebrity's new born baby.

I give up my indifference to words, my fingers positioned
on keyboard, I start typing, I hammer on keys, I write:
*"Each morning I flipped the newspaper thinking of you;
there is nothing that you missed."*

Signals

"Your index finger firm
on steel neck of the fork:
press your thumb tight
on its metal thigh.

Wrap around
the remaining three:
their nails diagonal
below the thumb.

And that is how
you also hold the knife.
Watch out that feeble
baby finger: keep it
stiff at all times.

Only females and homos
flash that finger
as they dine, sip wine."

Christopher knew well
how not to give away

any signals he was one
of the many he hated.

Asleep

He wipes kitchen shelves,
he polishes stoned floor;
throws all toys in the closet,
orders his boy to grow up.

Spends hours on the chaise,
watches drama films from 90s.
His boy runs round in circles
agitated for play, wife
too familiar to all sounds.

He forgets all his troubles,
forgets he's a father, forgets
about his wife, forgets
to eat and later falls asleep.

Nothingness

Angry at myself
for not having an answer:

why I wander and wander
and wander, reaching nowhere;

why I think and think
and think, but cannot think
another way of doing life.

I pause, I wait
another day, another hour;
nothingness   is a tiring job
in this body.

Dorothy Livesay

So gentle her words,
so subtle her discomfort
in pain; even resentment
decorated with sound,
dignity in spaces which
stand between words.

In the quiet of night,
I read her verses from
the unquiet bed: she laid
her hunger on the page,
never shy of body's longing;
always wanting
to be touched, heard
as a person.

Thirty Three

There are cobbled streets and pedestrian walks
for joy, for laughter, humour and banter
in this city.

No passages, no stalls, no showrooms,
no mannequins clad in skin tight jeans or
cashmere shawls selling pain, inviting sorrow.
No double glazed windows with signage
flashing desolation and loss.

*"In your message last week, you wrote
that you have not an hour's time
for sleep on some nights."*
I ask Conor; he creates silence.
His silence says: *"You are not allowed in.
Who are you, why may I confide in you?"*

Thirties can be a forlorn business,
no one prepares you for it; no one
trains you how to do it, how to think,
what to do when pain begins to form,
with no shops to go to, no leaflets to drop
to inform your friends of the loss of meaning,

loss of hope, separation from naivety.

"You are not allowed in, in
to the years I have lived, but this silence
I create, we both can inhabit and here
we can converse..." I listen,
Conor speaks.

Unimportant

Unimportant education, no degrees;
never a job, bedsheets and cutlery
is all she is. It is through food
she asserts her presence:

tangy ginger in cauliflower *roti*,
chopped coriander on onion salad;
in kidney beans curry, green chillies,
in chick peas gravy, black tea.

She asks you to eat and eat,
once and three times, until her food,
her love, her decades old presence,
her identity, her forlorn existence
settles down your stomach.

Shaila has spent her years in that
home, counting hours for her
husband to return, sleep together
before morning sets him free.

Each day, he goes away and she
becomes unseen, unimportant.

Deep

When a depth runs so deep
what measure could there be
no mind enough to perceive it.

When loneliness hits
brown earth below one's legs
fertile roots beneath the feet
all run deep.

Finding

The first time
a boy touched me intimately,
he said: *"Close your eyes
and now imagine
one day a girl will do this."*

The first time
I touched a woman unclothed,
we both liked it
and my friend took it away,
laughed.

The first time
I was told *"you are
not boy enough."*

First time
I danced with a girl, felt
a rush in my body.

First time
I longed for a kiss,
gave it a miss:

it was the week
before her wedding.

First time
I lay on bed with a man,
gazed at dimmed lights,
day dreamed and felt
this is beautiful.

Stopping

Stopping for the night:
he puts down the pages,
removes metal watch,
wallet remains in the front
pocket, pressed on thigh;
no glasses: tired eyes,
defeated mind.

There is more in his
day than what his
body could possess;
he lies on his bed
in the grey of the night,
a floor lamp points
to the wall on his right,
paints a round ball.

His fingers ruffle
through his brown hair:
one more day of life
might be a lot.

Counting Coins

She puts a government coin in the tin:
shakes it, feels it heavy, smiles;
her eyes desperate, lips hopeless.

"I do not want money," she says,
"I want to be happy."

Clara spends her days counting coins,
studying religion, baking cakes and
doing telephone calls.

When her boy returns from school,
errands and chores tow her away
from desolation.

Forty Seven

He had acquaintances of certain persuasions;
"all of them," he would say, *"had a situation."*

The men he liked were moody and erratic,
their demeanour flamboyant.

Christopher wanted men, but always kissed
his woman on the lips, to deny it in public.

His rehearsed manners never
let a signal slip.

Looking

I am more than neurosis and complexes,
an analysand with history and pain.

I am an ordinary man too; a pointless wanderer
finding liberation in nothingness.

"Look out the window... look far and wide!",
my friend Lola once said.

I have kept on looking.

Shoulder

Look at me, he says,
only four summers old
into this world.

Look at me, he says,
colours decking with
green and orange.

Look at me, he says,
runs round and round
the aluminium barbecue.

Look at me, he says,
slurps gherkin soup,
eats wet vermicelli.

Look at me, he says,
sprays jasmine scent
from sitting room to
upstairs bedroom.

Look at me, he says,
imitates a somersault,

finally cries, falls
asleep on mum's shoulder.

Tomorrow

– Give me two pounds sir,
I will find a home by tomorrow –

You can see him all day
asking for change: coins enough
to take him away from this wet
street of London.

Memory is a distant home:
he has forgotten we spoke
three months ago on a Saturday
in January outside an immigrant's
fries shop on the high street.

"Take 50p and telephone Shelter,
go to their office, they will
put you somewhere."

His memory always distant:
everyday he asks for change
from me, from old strangers,
hoping to find his home
by tomorrow.

Touch

You touched, you touched,
you touched.

I spoke, I spoke and spoke
how hollow I feel.

You kept on touching;
you never heard.

Jewellery

He leaves home each morning
half an hour after daylight; cuts through
office goers' traffic, spends his time
at the company; smokes cigarettes,
signs legal contracts.

Takes his wife few times a month
to get social with his colleagues; they eat
dinner, drink whisky with families.

Shaila takes few hours getting ready:
her only chance to be seen, to be known,
only chance to be admired.

She takes time to wear a *saree*;
time to chose a necklace; some time
to put on earrings; time to find
bangles; some time to fit in rings; time
to put on anklets.

Shaila and her make-up: those are
his only jewellery.

Weak

He sits in the drawing room,
oblivious to news and movies.
His wife flips channels, entertains
her mind ever empty in a menial life,
married to vegetables and crockery.

He has no inclination, no stories;
he is bankrupt of banter and emotion,
passion for politics or profession, he sits:
the only thing he does well.

He used to be a man of abuse:
powerless these days as his
arms grow weak.

Late

His hair so golden, so luminous:
never before have I watched
the Norwegian sun so close
and made my restlessness pause.

He lies on his father's lap,
scribbly paper dropped on floor.
He lies sheltered in the knowledge that
as the midnight sun flies over
Trondheim tonight, his arms
will flicker in sleep and he
will become a bird: three-year-olds
do not yet know names of
tiny little things with wings.

I watch them both in unbroken
sleep. The father holds his boy,
and the boy holds a passport:
pappa's liberty   to always be
a boy.

I want to be this boy tonight

Loss drowns slowly:
I am thirty years late.

Emptiness

Ramona lives in a newly lone house;
walnuts, apples, medlars and cherries
hang on the branches in her courtyard.

Neighbours, the homeless and
decades-old friends meet her at home,
watch her speak at rallies.

She tells me of the silence, of the emptiness:
I could never learn when it begins,
what is its origin.

If emptiness is that what is invisible,
I tell her, I and she

have lived invisible lives
with invisible companions all our years.

Loss

He irons white shirts,
hangs laundry in the verandah.

Wakes up after midnight, finds
chores to tire him.

Tidies grey book case
even though he knows

that all the books in this world
will not bring him happiness;

sweeps dust off stacked pages.
Loss is a moment, even after

death it finds a new life;
it doesn't end.

Counting

Few minutes each time
before she answered the doorbell.
When I entered her drawing room,
no hints or ashtrays, yet persistent
the smell of tobacco in that
air conditioned home: the lady
who smoked cigarettes in the
privacy of her hours, surrounded
by glass vases and classic literature,
said nothing about it.

I liked her drawing of a
vacant bench under a field maple
on a Wiltshire land, brought it home.
She once said it was dignity that she
lived twenty years without a man:
I count months and sometimes
too dejected of counting.

Coffee Date

Seated in a London café,
on a birch chair
by tall glass wall where
blue geraniums bloom,
he waits for a man
to arrive.

Sipping espresso
bitter on tongue
demands patience
to find what the
unknown man will hold.

He holds warm mug,
holds emotion,
holds memory;
yet he doesn't hold
what the hour does.

Ingram Content Group UK Ltd.
Milton Keynes UK
UKHW011455220523
422143UK00004B/37

9 780993 031526